our hope
and
expectation

DEVOTIONS FOR
ADVENT & CHRISTMAS
2020–2021

AUGSBURG FORTRESS

Minneapolis

OUR HOPE AND EXPECTATION
Devotions for Advent and Christmas 2020–2021

pISBN 978-1-5064-6782-5
eISBN 978-1-5064-7079-5

Writers: Paul E. Hoffman (November 29–December 5), Annabelle Markey (December 6–12), Michael Coffey (December 13–19), Rozella Haydée White (December 20–23), Troy M. Troftgruben (December 24–30), Pam Fickenscher (December 31–January 6)

Editor: Laurie J. Hanson
Cover image: Snow covered pine trees on sunset iStock/Tuutikka
Cover design: Alisha Lofgren
Interior design: Eileen Engebretson

Manufactured in the U.S.A.

Contents

Welcome

Our hope and expectation, O Jesus, now appear;
arise, O Sun so longed for, o'er this benighted sphere.
With hearts and hands uplifted, we plead, O Lord, to see
the day of earth's redemption that sets your people free!
—"Rejoice, rejoice, believers," ELW 244, st. 4

Our Hope and Expectation continues a centuries-old Christian tradition of setting aside time to prepare for the celebration of Jesus' birth and to anticipate his return. This Advent season of preparation then unfolds in the joy of the twelve days of Christmas and the day of Epiphany.

This book provides daily devotions for the first Sunday of Advent through Epiphany (November 29, 2020, through January 6, 2021). These devotions explore year B scripture readings (in the Revised Common Lectionary) for the Sundays of Advent and Christmas, as well as for the festival days of Christmas and Epiphany. Each reading is accompanied by a photo, a quote to ponder, a reflection, and a prayer. The book also offers household blessings and prayers (see pages 84-94) to enrich your preparations and celebrations.

May the hope and joy of the long-awaited Christ child be with you during the Advent and Christmas seasons!

Isaiah 64:1-2

O that you would tear open the heavens and come down,
so that the mountains would quake at your presence—
as when fire kindles brushwood
and the fire causes water to boil—
to make your name known to your adversaries,
so that the nations might tremble at your presence!

To ponder

The primary condition for a fruitful and rewarding Advent is
renunciation, surrender.—Alfred Delp, *The Prison Meditations of
Father Delp*

From our knees

What if we saw God tearing open the heavens, like so many light beams streaming through the cathedral skylight? That is the vision of the "Advent prophet," Isaiah, a vision both hopeful and terrifying.

I suspect that were this to happen, we would drop to our knees, which is exactly the place to begin this Advent journey. It's where the original hearers found themselves as Isaiah spoke these powerful, hopeful, and terrifying words. Having returned to the temple from exile, the people now cry out for things to be like they used to be, or at least the way people remember them.

Here on our knees, we surrender. We wait in humility and adoration, confession and anticipation. It's the perfect Advent posture.

As with Isaiah's people, we too come with memory and hope. The God who tears open the heavens is the same God who tears open the grave. It is difficult to know how such a God will come to life among us to challenge or change us. So from our knees we wait and watch, confident that the love that has sustained God's people in every Advent will also dawn upon us.

Prayer

O Jesus, we wait from our knees, in anticipation and awe, humility and hope. We wait in the confidence of your love, knowing that you have torn open the skies and made yourself known to us in the cross and empty tomb. Amen.

November 30

Isaiah 64:4

From ages past no one has heard,
no ear has perceived,
no eye has seen any God besides you,
who works for those who wait for him.

To ponder

How silently, how silently
the wondrous gift is giv'n! . . .
No ear can hear his coming;
but, in this world of sin,
where meek souls will receive him,
still the dear Christ enters in.
—"O little town of Bethlehem," ELW 279, st. 3

In unexpected places

Sometimes God's presence is so real that it cannot be mistaken. But often, it is more like prophet and poet describe: "no ear has perceived, no eye has seen"; "no ear can hear his coming."

One of Advent's gifts is pausing to sharpen our senses. In a chaotic, cacophonous world, we wait, and watch, and wonder. During this time-out, sometimes God's presence is so palpable that it cannot be mistaken. It is like Christ is standing on top of the world, arms outstretched, with hope and expectation. Advent is a season for us to sharpen our ears and eyes to see Jesus in less obvious places too. As we do, we will be awed by the one "who works for those who wait for him."

How silently Christ is visible with arms outstretched holding a cardboard sign on the freeway entrance ramp. No ear may hear him coming in the teenage voice crying out for environmental awareness, yet there Christ is. Where meek souls will receive him, Christ is visible in the plaintive eyes we encounter in the Alzheimer's wing.

Christ promises his presence in all of creation. By his rising, he ratifies that promise. Look for Jesus at all times and in all places. He will not disappoint.

Prayer

Lord Jesus, with outstretched arms you boldly come. In the silent, unexpected places, you come to us as well. We are grateful. Amen.

December 1

Psalm 80:1-3

Hear, O Shepherd of Israel, leading Joseph like a flock;
shine forth, you that are enthroned upon the cherubim.
In the presence of Ephraim, Benjamin, and Manasseh,
stir up your strength and come to help us.
Restore us, O God;
let your face shine upon us, and we shall be saved.

To ponder

Restore to me the joy of your salvation, and sustain me with your
bountiful spirit.—Psalm 51:12

[God] leads me beside still waters. You restore my soul, O Lord.
—Psalm 23:2-3

Restored right now by the Coming One

There we have it, a perfect trilogy of restoration: Psalms 23, 51, and 80. As sheep in need of care, we cry out with the ancient words of the psalmists on this Advent day. In hope and expectation, we pray that all that is broken will be restored.

This is not something we can do for ourselves. We are quite good at getting ourselves lost in aimlessness and adventures of our own making. Only the Coming One can rescue us from the brink and set us back on the path that leads by the still and holy waters.

These Advent days are busy days, hectic days, often anything-but-holy days. We may hear ourselves saying, "I just need to keep my head down and get through this, then Christmas will be here." It's in keeping our heads down that we get lost. But no need to wait until Christmas. Jesus the great restorer is with us now, and he will lead us home.

Prayer

Gracious Savior, leading us as a tender shepherd leads wandering sheep, help us to know your presence. When we get lost in the maze of busy-ness and too-full days, we trust you to restore us. Bring us back to you. Amen.

December 2

1 Corinthians 1:5-8

In every way you have been enriched in him, in speech and knowledge of every kind—just as the testimony of Christ has been strengthened among you—so that you are not lacking in any spiritual gift as you wait for the revealing of our Lord Jesus Christ. He will also strengthen you to the end, so that you may be blameless on the day of our Lord Jesus Christ.

To ponder

I believe that by my own understanding or strength I cannot believe in Jesus Christ my Lord or come to him.—Martin Luther, *Luther's Small Catechism*

Enriched, strengthened, and blameless

It's quite an assignment that 1 Corinthians 1 lays before us! To be enriched, strengthened, and blameless—who among us can make this happen, even for a nanosecond, before "the day of our Lord Jesus Christ"?

Ah, but we are not the ones to make this happen. Each of those qualities is connected to Christ. We wait in hope and expectation, not for the completion of our self-improvement projects, but for the One who makes it possible for us to be enriched, strengthened, and blameless and to stand before him. These are not qualities we dig deep within ourselves to produce. These are gifts given by the loving Christ.

No need to wait for Christ's so-called second coming to step into the enrichment, strength, and blamelessness God gives every day. *Today* is a day of the coming of Christ. By our baptism Jesus lives among us, so we can go into the world right here, right now, confident of having all we need to love and serve those around us.

Prayer

Gracious Jesus, you are an endless giver. You give us all we need each and every day to bring your love to those in need around us. Remind us in this day that you are with us, and that through your presence we are called to serve. Amen.

December 3

Mark 13:24-26

[Jesus said:]
"But in those days, after that suffering,
the sun will be darkened,
and the moon will not give its light,
and the stars will be falling from heaven,
and the powers in the heavens will be shaken.
Then they will see 'the Son of Man coming in clouds' with great
power and glory."

To ponder

My Lord, what a morning; my Lord, what a morning;
oh, my Lord, what a morning, when the stars begin to fall.
—"My Lord, what a morning," ELW 438, refrain

Falling stars are everywhere

No need to look to the sky in search of falling stars—they are all around us. The sky is falling every day.

Stars fall from the sky with every act of hatred or injustice. The sky is falling when one faction seeks domination over another. Sometimes stars burn out on a less cosmic level. They fall when we disappoint one another or ourselves, when a diagnosis is revealed, when a child is bullied.

But stars belong in the hand of the one who created them. Their falling is never the end of the story. Listen: *You will see the Son of Man coming in clouds with great power and glory.*

Our days are a combination of falling stars and the Son of Man coming. In this season of hope and expectation, Christ's coming will always be more glorious than any stars of ours that fall. After all, it is by his hands that they first were formed. By his hand they will be hung again in a sky that never dims.

Prayer

Lord Jesus, you were there when the foundations of the world were laid, when the stars were hung in the heavens. Remind us that, whatever stars may fall around us, your love for your creation is endless. Through that love, give us hope. Amen.

December 4

Mark 13:30-31

[Jesus said:] "Truly I tell you, this generation will not pass away until all these things have taken place. Heaven and earth will pass away, but my words will not pass away."

To ponder

In the beginning was the Word, and the Word was with God, and the Word was God.—John 1:1

God's toolkit

It is nothing short of amazing that God's toolkit at creation had nothing in it other than God's word. God spoke and it was done. *Let there be light!*

One would think it could never get more amazing than that. But—wait for it—when God knew that the time was right, God one-upped us. God *became* the Word, and "lived among us . . . full of grace and truth" (John 1:14).

Jesus is that living Word, the one for whom we wait in these Advent days of hope and expectation. Today's scripture text gives us a hint about just how spectacular this living Word will be for us. Jesus is the Word that will not pass away.

There's a lot of Easter in Advent, and today is a perfect example. Not just anyone can promise that one's word will abide forever. But Jesus can, because of his Easter victory over death. He lives forever. He gives us life forever. He is the living Word, the perfect instrument in God's eternal toolkit. He who was in the beginning will never pass away.

Prayer

Lord Jesus, living Word, the world teaches us that nothing lasts forever. But your teaching is more perfect and more powerful, sealed by your resurrection. Your word lasts forever, and on that word we anchor all our hope. Amen.

December 5

Mark 13:32, 35-37

[Jesus said:] "But about that day or hour no one knows, neither the angels in heaven, nor the Son, but only the Father. . . . Therefore, keep awake—for you do not know when the master of the house will come, in the evening, or at midnight, or at cock-crow, or at dawn, or else he may find you asleep when he comes suddenly. And what I say to you I say to all: Keep awake."

To ponder

We, who are many, are one body in Christ, and individually we are members one of another.—Romans 12:5

What if we take turns?

Keep awake? Few things are harder than to stay awake when one is exhausted. The body cries out for rest, just as it does with hunger or thirst. The writer of Mark must not know the latest research regarding the importance of a full eight hours of sleep each night. We need to sleep, and no amount of exhortation from Mark will change that. What's the watchful follower of Jesus to do?

We sometimes forget that Mark was writing to a community, not to individual Christians. We too are baptized into community. We do not belong to ourselves: "We are members one of another." So let's take turns. You stay awake while I sleep. When we're both exhausted, we'll tap another to keep watch for us. And when she is tired, you or I can step up.

We were made for community, intended to work together. Our waiting and watching are best when shared. In that sharing we will find our hope and expectation, Advent joy.

Prayer

Dear God, you created us to live in community with you and with one another. There is too much for any one of us to do on our own. Help us to find the joy of taking turns, and in that beautiful rotation to be found by you. Amen.

2 Peter 3:8-9

Do not ignore this one fact, beloved, that with the Lord one day
is like a thousand years, and a thousand years are like one day.
The Lord is not slow about his promise, as some think of slow-
ness, but is patient with you, not wanting any to perish, but all to
come to repentance.

To ponder

Have patience with everything that remains unsolved in your
heart. Try to love the questions themselves, like locked rooms and
like books written in a foreign language. Do not now look for the
answers. They cannot now be given to you because you could not
live them. It is a question of experiencing everything. At present

you need to live the question. Perhaps you will gradually, without even noticing it, find yourself experiencing the answer, some distant day.—Rainer Maria Rilke, *Letters to a Young Poet*

God's patience

Those who first heard these words of scripture were having a hard time being patient. Jesus was supposed to return soon—and he hadn't. There were growing pains and risks as they struggled to discern how to live as followers of Christ in a Greco-Roman pagan world. But the author of 2 Peter insists there's a reason for the Lord's delay. God wants all to come to repentance—to take on a new mind, a change of heart, or a new perspective.

Patiently waiting, brimming with questions, longing for answers, hoping desperately to glimpse change in the world and in ourselves is not easy. However, in practicing patience and attentiveness, and in loving "the questions themselves," we grow as followers of Christ. This is not because our salvation rests on it, but because God wants us to more deeply experience the fullness of our acceptance and forgiveness in Christ. As we grow and learn, others can experience Christ at work in and through us.

With what unanswered question are you wrestling? How might you offer it to God in prayer as you await Christ's coming?

Prayer

Holy One, help us to be patient as we wait for you and offer you our questions and our lives each day. Amen.

December 7

2 Peter 3:13-15

In accordance with [God's] promise, we wait for new heavens and a new earth, where righteousness is at home. Therefore, beloved, while you are waiting for these things, strive to be found by him at peace, without spot or blemish; and regard the patience of our Lord as salvation.

To ponder

Christian community is not an ideal we have to realize, but rather a reality created by God in Christ in which we may participate. The more clearly we learn to recognize that the ground and strength and promise of all our community is in Jesus Christ alone, the more calmly we will learn to think about our community and pray and hope for it.—Dietrich Bonhoeffer, *Life Together*

22

Waiting with the family of God

My two brothers and I loved sledding. We'd fling ourselves on our inner tubes and head down the hill in the backyard, squealing with glee. Inevitably, however, we'd start building snow forts—and if anyone messed up another's creation, it wasn't a pretty picture.

Community is like that. It's fun and joyful and creative until . . . it's not. Egos and pride, self-righteousness and simple misunderstandings get in the way faster than you can throw a snowball.

So we wait in hope for God's kingdom to take over. Empowered by the Holy Spirit working within and among us, in a blessed community of sinners/saints, we seek to love as Christ loved us. We confess and forgive, practice vulnerability and trust, and humbly surrender our egos for the sake of our siblings in Christ. We focus on the incredible gift that is life together, learning from, supporting, and encouraging one another in our faith journeys. Life together is the gift God has given—a diverse group of people drawn together from all backgrounds, experiences, cultures, races, ethnicities, genders, orientations, and so on—for the sake of sharing the good news of Jesus Christ in our world.

Prayer

Christ, you alone are our hope. May we celebrate and rejoice in the amazing gift of community you have given us to share in this good news! Amen.

Isaiah 40:1-2

Comfort, O comfort my people, says your God.
Speak tenderly to Jerusalem, and cry to her
that she has served her term, that her penalty is paid,
that she has received from the LORD's hand double for all her sins.

To ponder

"Comfort, comfort now my people;
tell of peace!" So says our God.
Comfort those who sit in darkness
mourning under sorrow's load.
To God's people now proclaim
that God's pardon waits for them!

Tell them that their war is over;
God will reign in peace forever.
—"Comfort, comfort now my people," ELW 256, st. 1

What becomes of the brokenhearted?

God's people Israel had been in exile, living in a foreign land, yearning for home and the life they had known. But God was not done with them! The Lord announces to all heaven and earth that the time of sadness is over. God remains their God and will bind up their wounds. They may have sought after idols and failed to uphold their part of the covenant, but God will never revoke God's promises. The Faithful One will reestablish them.

We have all made mistakes and sinned. We've ruptured relationships with others, with creation, and with God. We've participated, by sins of commission or omission, in the systemic "-isms" of our time—racism, ageism, consumerism, and so on. We have much to confess and repent of. We've caused and received heartache through our own egos and brokenness.

Still, the Most High calls out for comfort for all the people of God. God speaks tenderly to us, proclaiming that our time of heartache and exile shall not last forever. Nothing and no one can banish us from God's abundant love and grace. We have a place as God's beloved people today and forever.

Prayer

God of faithfulness, even in our suffering and heartache, you bring us tender comfort. Thank you, Lord. Amen.

December 9

Isaiah 40:3-5
"In the wilderness prepare the way of the Lord,
make straight in the desert a highway for our God.
Every valley shall be lifted up,
and every mountain and hill be made low;
the uneven ground shall become level,
and the rough places a plain.
Then the glory of the Lord shall be revealed,
and all people shall see it together,
for the mouth of the Lord has spoken."

To ponder
Then fling the gates wide open to greet your promised king!
Your king, yet ev'ry nation its tribute too may bring.

26

All lands will bow before him; their voices join your singing:
Hosanna to the Lord, for he fulfills God's word!
—"Prepare the royal highway," ELW 264, st. 3

A wild road traveled together

Sometimes it's hard to visualize things when they are described
to you. There can also be a disconnect between what we picture
in our minds and the reality. When the Lord returns, however,
all people will be able to see it. In the wild and parched places,
straight through valleys and mountains, a smooth pathway for
God will be revealed. God will come onto the scene without
any hindrance. Are we prepared to receive God into our lives so
readily, or do we need some "roadside assistance"?

Sometimes there's a disconnect between how we expect God
to come to us and what encountering God is really like. I've found
it's more often in the unexpected places, in the wildernesses, in
the confusion and pain, in sorrows as well as joys that I encounter
the triune God most clearly. This is the way of the cross—God
with us in a manger and on a tree, God who journeys with us in
the wilderness.

Prayer

God-with-us, open our hearts so we perceive you on our journey
in the wilderness of our lives. Smooth out the rough places in us
so we can prepare a way for you in our world. Amen.

December 10

Isaiah 40:11

He will feed his flock like a shepherd;
he will gather the lambs in his arms,
and carry them in his bosom,
and gently lead the mother sheep.

To ponder

Good Shepherd, You have a wild and crazy sheep in love with
thorns and brambles. But please don't get tired of looking for me!
I know You won't. For You have found me. All I have to do is stay
found.—Thomas Merton, *A Book of Hours*

A tender strength

One summer I had the opportunity to bottle-feed baby goats (kids). It was sweet and tender, rather rambunctious, and very funny. However, what surprised me was the ferocity of these adorable creatures as they sucked down nourishment. When the farmer handed out the bottles, we learned not to stand between the kids and their food!

God leads people back from exile, gathering them up and carrying them home to the land of milk and honey. In the Hebrew Scriptures, God and kings are frequently referred to using this pastoral imagery, but shepherds also need a strong hand. They need to be able to lead and guide, to protect and shelter, all out of an abundance of love for those in their care.

As you wait and prepare for Christ, how do you need to experience the gentle but firm leading of the Good Shepherd? Are there places where you are seeking God's tenderness? What about situations where you need the wisdom and guidance of the One willing to lay down his life for his sheep? Come. The Shepherd waits to gather you in his arms.

Prayer

Good Shepherd, carry us gently as we wait for you, turning our hearts from all that doesn't feed and nurture us, toward you, who have fed and tended us with your very self. Amen.

Mark 1:1-3

The beginning of the good news of Jesus Christ, the Son of God.
As it is written in the prophet Isaiah,
"See, I am sending my messenger ahead of you,
who will prepare your way;
the voice of one crying out in the wilderness:
'Prepare the way of the Lord, make his paths straight.'"

To ponder

We cannot do everything, and there is a sense of liberation in realizing that. This enables us to do something, and to do it very well . . . . We may never see the end results, but that is the difference between the master builder and the worker. We are workers, not master builders; ministers, not messiahs. We are prophets of

a future not our own.—Ken Untener, "Prophets of a Future Not
Our Own"

Everyday prophets

Advent is this beautiful time of waiting for the coming of our
Savior at Christmas. But it is not a time to sit around twiddling
our thumbs. We are to be intentional. This is a time of active
waiting, engaging with the world around us, and preparing our
hearts and minds to receive the God who comes to us, not only
on Christmas amid candles and carols, but in the mundane messi-
ness of each and every day.

Mark's gospel is not one to dillydally. Instead the author jumps
right into the action, declaring this the beginning of the good
news! As we hear about John the baptizer, there's another urgency
rising to the surface: How will *you* prepare not only your heart
but the world around you to hear the good news? We are called to
share the good news, but so often we stammer about our inability
to do so. We fear rejection or even being ignored as irrelevant.
Mark's gospel and Advent call us to train, to prepare, to share this
life-giving news; to make forgiveness, love, and mercy the words
on our lips and the work of our hands, feet, and hearts. We may
not see the fruits of our labor, but how will we joyfully participate
in the future God is building?

Prayer

Builder of the future, what an awesome gift and responsibility you
have given to us—to be part of the work you are doing. Amen.

December 12

Mark 1:4-5

John the baptizer appeared in the wilderness, proclaiming a baptism of repentance for the forgiveness of sins. And people from the whole Judean countryside and all the people of Jerusalem were going out to him, and were baptized by him in the river Jordan, confessing their sins.

To ponder

Do not be ashamed to enter again into the Church. . . . Do not be ashamed when you repent. . . . These are two things: sin and repentance. Sin is a wound; repentance is a medicine. Just as there are for the body wounds and medicines, so for the soul are sins and repentance. However, sin has the shame and repentance possesses the courage.—John Chrysostom, *Homily 8*

We begin again

Over the past few years, I have been discovering the importance and beauty of practicing individual confession and forgiveness. I cherish corporate confession and absolution and I firmly believe God hears me when I confess in silence, but I have come to realize the power of speaking my sins aloud to a trusted sibling in Christ. This may sound horrifying, but admitting something and bringing it into the light helps to take away some of the power it holds, to begin cleaning out those wounds we all carry and inflict, to hear with new ears that we are forgiven.

To repent means more than feeling badly about what we've done. It means to "turn around" or "get a new mind" (*metanoia*) about something. Repentance is being re-formed by God's grace and forgiveness to live into the new life we have in Christ.

As you run around getting ready for holiday parties and family gatherings; buying, making, and wrapping presents; cooking meals and baking cookies, stress can run awfully high. Chances are there may be some stress-induced moments when you aren't, let's just say, your "best self." How can this time of waiting be a time to reframe things? To get a new mind and start over again? How can this be a time to adopt a new perspective about what is truly important and meaningful, and to let the rest go?

Prayer

Gracious God, over and over you give us clean hearts and new perspectives. I confess my sins before you. Help me start again and return to you. Thank you for your forgiveness. Amen.

33

December 13 / Advent 3

John 1:6-9

There was a man sent from God, whose name was John. He came as a witness to testify to the light, so that all might believe through him. He himself was not the light, but he came to testify to the light. The true light, which enlightens everyone, was coming into the world.

To ponder

Be thou my vision, O Lord of my heart;
naught be all else to me, save that thou art:
thou my best thought both by day and by night,
waking or sleeping, thy presence my light.
—"Be thou my vision," ELW 793, st. 1

Reflectors

When I was a kid, I rode my bike everywhere. In the days before mandated bike helmets, our biggest safety accessories were headlights and reflectors (white on the front and red on the back). I thought the headlight on my ten-speed was great, except it took batteries. Since I never remembered to replace the batteries, the headlight never worked. The reflectors, though, always worked. When light shone on them, they reflected it back and out. It is amazing how much light they could reflect and how bright they could be.

John was called to point the way to Christ, to reflect the light of Jesus. It may have been tempting to be a headlight and shine with his own light, but John knew that he was not the light. He was a witness to the light, a sign, a reflector shining in the light of Christ.

We too are called to reflect the light of Christ, not to be a headlight. This is no small thing. Reflectors shine bright when such brilliant light is shining on them.

Prayer

O God, give us such a vision of your love in Jesus that we reflect the light of your grace to everyone we meet today. Amen.

December 14

John 1:19-21

This is the testimony given by John when the Jews sent priests and Levites from Jerusalem to ask him, "Who are you?" He confessed and did not deny it, but confessed, "I am not the Messiah." And they asked him, "What then? Are you Elijah?" He said, "I am not." "Are you the prophet?" He answered, "No."

To ponder

Who am I? This or the other? Am I one person today, and tomorrow another? Am I both at once? A hypocrite before others, and before myself a contemptibly woebegone weakling? Or is something within me still like a beaten army, fleeing in disorder from victory already achieved?

Who am I? They mock me, these lonely questions of mine.

Whoever I am, Thou knowest, O God, I am thine.—Dietrich Bonhoeffer, *Letters and Papers from Prison*

Free to be me

As a child I loved the songs, short stories, and teachings in the "Free to Be . . . You and Me" program created by Marlo Thomas. It gave children permission to be themselves. One shortcoming in the program, and in the general focus on "being yourself" in our culture, however, is the assumption that we know who we are. Many of us struggle much of our lives to answer that question. Often we have to accept who we are *not*, as much as who we are.

John the Baptist seems like the kind of person who figured out who he was, perhaps through years of deep spiritual reflection, testing, and prayer. In today's scripture reading we hear one other important part of John figuring out who he was: knowing who he was not. He was important, but not the Messiah. He was beloved of God, and that was enough.

Who are you? Start with "beloved of God." Let go of who you are not. Trust that you are God's and you will be free to be you— even as you spend your life figuring out exactly what that means.

Prayer

O God, you know who I am. Help me to trust my belovedness in you, and to honor the belovedness in everyone I encounter today. Amen.

December 15

John 1:24-27

Now [the priests and Levites] had been sent from the Pharisees. They asked [John], "Why then are you baptizing if you are neither the Messiah, nor Elijah, nor the prophet?" John answered them, "I baptize with water. Among you stands one whom you do not know, the one who is coming after me; I am not worthy to untie the thong of his sandal."

To ponder

True humility does not know that it is humble. If it did, it would be proud from the contemplation of so fine a virtue.—Martin Luther, in *Martin Luther's Christmas Book*

Humility trap

An organization wanted to give an award to the most humble person. But every person who received the award became so proud that the award had to be taken away! What happens when you know you are more humble than others? Pride sets in. Humility collapses.

Many believed John the Baptist was one of the greatest teachers. People came from all over to hear him and be baptized by him. Kings were curious about him and wanted to meet him. One day some people were sent out to the river to meet John. He was proclaiming the opportunity for a new start with God, so they thought he was great. You can imagine how easily all of this could have gone to John's head.

But John had already said he wasn't a prophet, or Elijah returned, or the Messiah. He said someone was coming who was greater than he. John became humble, not to win the Humility Olympics, but because he knew the coming Messiah was great.

When we seek to lift up Christ as the truly great one from God, we have no need to elevate ourselves or compare ourselves to others. We know that Jesus' greatness leads to our belovedness.

Prayer

Holy One, give us true humility so we can show forth your greatness. Amen.

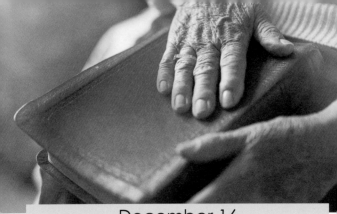

December 16

1 Thessalonians 5:16-19, 23

Rejoice always, pray without ceasing, give thanks in all circumstances; for this is the will of God in Christ Jesus for you. Do not quench the Spirit. . . . May the God of peace himself sanctify you entirely; and may your spirit and soul and body be kept sound and blameless at the coming of our Lord Jesus Christ.

To ponder

Gratitude is not about stuff. Gratitude is the emotional response to the surprise of our very existence, to sensing that inner light and realizing the astonishing sacred, social, and scientific events that brought each one of us into being. We cry out like the psalmist, "I am fearfully and wonderfully made!" (Ps. 139:14).—Diana Butler Bass, *Grateful: The Subversive Practice of Giving Thanks*

40

In all circumstances?

Years ago my mother suffered from stage IV lung cancer. It's a terrible disease. When she got the diagnosis, we knew she had one to two years to live, and part of that time included the awful side effects of chemotherapy.

To cope with what was happening to her during her illness, she wrote a note to her cancer— thanking it. Why did she do this? Not because she was grateful for her circumstances, but because through her illness she learned to trust that she was more deeply loved by her family and friends and God than she ever knew before.

We are not expected to give thanks *for* all of our circumstances, but *in* all our circumstances we can give thanks—thanks to God for life and love, thanks to others who make our lives rich, thanks for dogs and cats and trees and flowers and herbs and air and stars.

When we give thanks in all circumstances, we resist the temptation to lose sight of God's love and grace. We insist that life is a gift, no matter what, no matter how short.

Prayer

God of all gifts, make us grateful in all circumstances that we are eternally loved. Amen.

December 17

Isaiah 61:1-2

The spirit of the Lord God is upon me,
because the Lord has anointed me;
he has sent me to bring good news to the oppressed,
to bind up the brokenhearted,
to proclaim liberty to the captives,
and release to the prisoners;
to proclaim the year of the Lord's favor.

To ponder

Lift every voice and sing till earth and heaven ring,
ring with the harmonies of liberty.
—"Lift every voice and sing," ELW 841, st. 1

Liberating liberty

Isaiah celebrates the good news of God's liberation, healing, and comfort. This good news is for all suffering under oppression, illness, and hopelessness; and for all hoping for release from the struggles that diminish their lives and their loved ones' lives. All can trust in what God is doing through God's prophets and people.

There is another liberation happening in this text and in these prophetic actions. Not only are those who have been oppressed and broken given new life, but those who participate in liberating and healing others are also set free. No one is truly free until everyone is free. There is no true liberation unless everyone is liberated.

Jesus read the Isaiah text aloud at the beginning of his ministry. He invited his disciples to join him in healing, blessing, forgiving—and in ending oppression. Even Jesus could not live the fullness of life God intended for him unless he worked for the fullness of life for all.

In the church too are people who need liberation and people who work for the liberation of others. All receive the gift of living in the freedom of God's grace in Christ.

Prayer

God of liberating grace, set us free from complacent and uncaring hearts so we can set others free to live a blessed life together in you. Amen.

December 18

Isaiah 61:10

I will greatly rejoice in the LORD,
my whole being shall exult in my God;
for he has clothed me with the garments of salvation.

To ponder

Let us rise up completely new
with the garments of justice on.
Living fully in Christ we'll bloom
in that sweet and delightful dawn.
Like the threads of a tapestry,
oh, let us unite in love.

And weave a joyful community
as we welcome the reign of God.
—Bret Hesla, "Let Us Put On the Clothes of Christ," st. 4

A favorite shirt

I had a favorite shirt a few years ago that I wore for years. It was light blue with a dark blue abstract floral design. Somehow just wearing it felt good. One day the shirt got washed with my fountain pen still in the pocket. It ended up covered in ink stains, and that was the end of it.

In the church we celebrate that Christ brings us salvation, and as Isaiah says, that gift is like a garment, a robe, a colorful accessory, a shining jewel. This gift of love and life in Christ can become our favorite shirt to wear every day to remind ourselves that we are God's beloved through baptism into Christ. This is what makes us rejoice deep in our hearts. When we live every day wearing this kind of deep joy, we experience life differently. We can be truly present to ourselves and others, accepting who we are and who they are. Like Isaiah, we "greatly rejoice" in God.

Prayer

Clothe me in your garments of salvation, merciful God, so daily I rejoice in you. Amen.

December 19

Isaiah 61:11

For as the earth brings forth its shoots,
and as a garden causes what is sown in it to spring up,
so the Lord God will cause righteousness and praise
to spring up before all the nations.

To ponder

Your Word, O Lord, is gentle dew
to suff'ring hearts that want it;
oh, shed your heav'nly balm anew,
to all your garden grant it;
refreshed by you, may ev'ry tree

bud forth and blossom gaily
and fruit and seed bring daily.
—*Lutheran Book of Worship* 232, st. 1

My herb garden

I have a hydroponic herb garden. I love to cook with fresh herbs, so when I need some basil or oregano or chives, I just snip some off. Recently I seeded new herbs. As the plants grew, I realized that the large leaves sprouting in the spot for thyme did not look like thyme. I tasted them—green apple-ish and lemony—not thyme. I didn't know what it was, but friends told me it was sorrel. Not what I expected, but I was happy to cook with something I had never used before.

God causes praise to spring up from the garden of the world by sowing justice, mercy, and forgiveness—and often where we least expect it. We assume the world will continue to cultivate greed, mistrust, and oppression. Or we just assume the world will operate as we have known it, and if it works for us, we're fine with that. But God will keep bringing forth shoots that give life to all. As people of faith we join with everyone moved to praise God for God's unexpected garden of justice and mercy that continues to sprout among us from Christ's life and love.

Prayer

Life-giving God, refresh us with your garden of love, and move us always to give you praise. Amen.

December 20 / Advent 4

Psalm 89:1

Your love, O LORD, forever will I sing;
from age to age my mouth
will proclaim your faithfulness.

To ponder

To acknowledge our ancestors means we are aware that we did
not make ourselves, that the line stretches all the way back,
perhaps to God; or to Gods. We remember them because it is an
easy thing to forget: that we are not the first to suffer, rebel, fight,
love and die. The grace with which we embrace life, in spite of the
pain, the sorrow, is always a measure of what has gone before.
—Alice Walker, "Fundamental Difference"

Take the long view

God's love and steadfastness endure, transcending boundaries of time and place, and flowing throughout the generations. When I think about what I know to be true about God, I need to take the long view. This view of God's steadfastness and love is informed by the stories, struggles, and triumphs of my ancestors, from those who survived the "middle passage" and the transatlantic slave trade, to those who migrated from Puerto Rico, to those who somehow managed to make a life for future generations despite Reconstruction and Jim Crow and systemic and structural evil that oppressed my ancestors simply because of the color of their skin or the language they spoke.

When I take this long view, I understand how the psalmist could sing of God's love and tell the story of God's faithfulness to all generations. The lives and experiences of my ancestors point to a God who has healed, protected, uplifted, empowered, and loved a people out of bondage and into liberation. I cannot help but praise God when I think about the lives of my ancestors and who I have become. Their expectant hope was passed on to me and, because of what I have witnessed, I too will sing of God's steadfast love and faithfulness throughout the generations.

Prayer

Creator God, help us to take the long view; to learn from those who have lived and loved before us; and to trust that you are still creating, redeeming, and loving. Amen.

December 21

2 Samuel 7:8-9, 16

Now therefore thus you shall say to my servant David: Thus says the LORD of hosts: I took you from the pasture, from following the sheep to be prince over my people Israel; and I have been with you wherever you went, and have cut off all your enemies from before you; and I will make for you a great name. . . . Your house and your kingdom shall be made sure forever before me; your throne shall be established forever.

To ponder

You are moving in the direction of freedom and the function of freedom is to free someone else.—Toni Morrison, Barnard College Commencement Speech, 1979

Lean into liberation

God called David from a seemingly ordinary life into an extraordinary purpose. The prophet Nathan shared God's expansive vision with David, a vision that David would work for the liberation of the people of Israel—people who had suffered and wandered and wondered about life as they sought the promised land. Liberation would not be just for the time of David's reign, but for generations to come. David's role was to be faithful and trust the promises of God, who had been steadfast in supporting and protecting David and the people.

What we do, how we live, and who we love will impact future generations. One thing that my faith and the stories of my ancestors have taught me is that I am responsible for sharing my gifts and honoring my call in ways that bring others along on this journey of life, liberation, and love. The gifts and experiences I have been given are not simply for me. They are for the collective. We are called as individuals whose gifts are nurtured by the Creator to bear witness to God's vision of liberation and love.

How is God calling you to use your gifts to bring about liberation for others?

Prayer

Liberating God, we thank you for the freedom found in you. We thank you for the ways that you call us and give us everything we need to serve you and love each other. Amen.

December 22

Luke 1:26-31

The angel Gabriel was sent by God to a town in Galilee called Nazareth, to a virgin engaged to a man whose name was Joseph, of the house of David. . . . And he came to her and said, "Greetings, favored one! The Lord is with you." But she was much perplexed by his words and pondered what sort of greeting this might be. The angel said to her, "Do not be afraid, Mary, for you have found favor with God. And now, you will conceive in your womb and bear a son, and you will name him Jesus."

To ponder

When we drop fear, we can draw nearer to people, we can draw nearer to the earth, we can draw nearer to all the heavenly creatures that surround us.—bell hooks, "bell hooks and John Perry Barlow talk"

Let go of fear

What was Mary thinking and feeling when the angel Gabriel greeted her? Being visited by an angel was one thing, but the message that Gabriel had for her—something totally different! Mary's entire world was about to change and the path before her could only be traversed with faith, hope, and love.

Fear is not inherently a bad thing—it can warn us of danger and cause us to be more cautious. It leads many of us, however, to fight, flee, or freeze; to question our identity and ability; or to lash out at those around us. Fear grows when we believe the lies it peddles—that we aren't good enough, that there isn't enough, that people won't care enough. Out of fear we build barriers and remain isolated from ourselves and each other.

Love leads us out of ourselves and moves us to create bridges instead of barriers. As we let go of fear and lean into love, we become curious and open to what's being revealed. Love beckons us closer to each other and leads us into wonder.

When was the last time you let go of fear and leaned into love?

Prayer

Sustaining God, you have not given us a spirit of fear but a spirit of power and of love and of sound mind. Inspire us to be curious and to seek out the deeper meanings and messages held in our encounters with you and with each other. Amen.

December 23

Luke 1:38

Mary said, "Here am I, the servant of the Lord; let it be with me according to your word." Then the angel departed from her.

To ponder

There are years that ask questions and years that answer.—Zora Neale Hurston, *Their Eyes Were Watching God*

Live in faith

To live in faith is to take the long view, to lean into liberation, and to let go of fear. To live in faith is to say yes to God, especially when you don't know where that yes will lead. To live in faith is to lean in and not pull back. To live in faith is hard; we all need support to embody lives of faith, hope, and love. To live in faith

54

is to be courageous and to follow the wisdom of the Divine who calls you into a future not yet known.

Mary decided to live in faith. I believe that her openness to the road ahead was informed by ancestral wisdom, the people and stories of faith passed down to her that revealed a God who was constantly present and providing guidance and support to those who were faithful. Ancestral wisdom was poured into Mary and being born of Mary, because she was open to it and to the Divine's calling.

There have been times when I lived in fear and not in faith, when I focused only on what I could see; held onto thoughts, ideas, and relationships that were oppressive; and believed the lie of scarcity. Living in fear, however, does not honor the ancestral wisdom of our past or waiting to be born. Living in faith opens us up to a long line of ancestors in faith who strengthen us, through the power of the Holy Spirit, to lean into moments when God is beckoning us to say yes and to say, "Here I am."

Mary said yes and the world was blessed. The ancestors rejoiced and future generations came to faith because of the story that unfolded through her.

What does living in faith look like for you?

Prayer

God of all life, we give you thanks for the gift of faith that beckons us to live lives of vision, liberation, and courage. May we continue in the long line of those who, despite fear and confusion, said yes to you. Amen.

December 24 / Christmas Eve

Luke 2:1-7

In those days a decree went out from Emperor Augustus that all the world should be registered. This was the first registration and was taken while Quirinius was governor of Syria. All went to their own towns to be registered. Joseph also went from the town of Nazareth in Galilee to Judea, to the city of David called Bethlehem, because he was descended from the house and family of David. He went to be registered with Mary, to whom he was engaged and who was expecting a child. While they were there, the time came for her to deliver her child. And she gave birth to her firstborn son and wrapped him in bands of cloth, and laid him in a manger, because there was no place for them in the inn.

To ponder

Silent night, holy night! Son of God, love's pure light.—"Silent night, holy night," ELW 281, st. 3

The sacredness of the unexpected

Luke's Christmas story may be so familiar that it's hard to imagine it differently. But Mary and Joseph probably did not envision things this way: an administrative census, a mid-travel birth, no guestroom vacancies, a not-so-silent night, and a nursery inhabited by animals. Not exactly a new parent's dream.

When our firstborn son arrived, things also did not go as planned for my wife and me. He showed up three weeks early, in the middle of the night, just days before Christmas. Our apartment was not ready. Our family members were not ready. We were not ready. Our newborn-arrival plans got revised. And we spent Christmas that year in a hospital room, eating off plastic trays, sporting multicolored lights and Santa hats, just the three of us.

To this day, it is the most sacred and special Christmas we have known. We learned that God's presence is prone to show up through the unexpected, the unwelcome, and the untraditional. Funny, many of us work hard to keep our Christmas traditions unchanged. But God's greatest Gift often comes to us through the things that don't go as planned.

Prayer

O Christ child, let us welcome you into our homes, our lives, and our hearts, especially when you show up unexpectedly. Amen.

December 25 / Christmas Day

Luke 2:8-14

In that region there were shepherds living in the fields, keeping watch over their flock by night. Then an angel of the Lord stood before them, and the glory of the Lord shone around them, and they were terrified. But the angel said to them, "Do not be afraid; for see—I am bringing you good news of great joy for all the people: to you is born this day in the city of David a Savior, who is the Messiah, the Lord. This will be a sign for you: you will find a child wrapped in bands of cloth and lying in a manger." And suddenly there was with the angel a multitude of the heavenly host, praising God and saying, "Glory to God in the highest heaven, and on earth peace among those whom he favors!"

To ponder

He is the Savior. . . . let everything else go.—Martin Luther, "Sermon on the Afternoon of Christmas Day" (1530)

To *you* is born *this day* . . .

Christmas Day celebrates the birth of Jesus. For many of us, news of this event is familiar and traditional. It may not feel new or startling. It may even seem like ancient history. After all, peace on earth feels more distant from our day than near at hand.

But the angel's words bar this message from confinement to the past: "To you is born this day. . ." The Savior's birth is not just historic—it is *for you*, reading and hearing this news right now. And although first spoken long ago, the promise is for *this day* no less than for then. Whatever you think about Christ's birth, the angel reminds you: it is truly *for you today*.

Martin Luther once wrote: "The chief article and foundation of the gospel is that before you take Christ as an example, you accept and recognize him as a gift, as a present that God has given you and that is your own" ("Brief Instruction," 1521). That thought alone may occupy our hearts today: Christ is for you, born for you, for you this day.

Prayer

O Christ our Savior, let us receive you as God's gift this day. Glory to God in the highest heaven, and on earth peace to all. Amen.

December 26

Luke 2:16-19

[The shepherds] went with haste and found Mary and Joseph, and the child lying in the manger. When they saw this, they made known what had been told them about this child; and all who heard it were amazed at what the shepherds told them. But Mary treasured all these words and pondered them in her heart.

To ponder

Infant holy, infant lowly, for his bed a cattle stall;
oxen lowing, little knowing Christ the child is Lord of all.
—"Infant holy, infant lowly," ELW 276, st. 1

Mary, did you know?

A familiar Christmas song asks the question, "Mary, did you know?" Luke's gospel implies she knew quite a bit. Months beforehand, Mary foresaw that "all generations will call me blessed" because of this child, who will scatter the proud, lift up the lowly, fill the hungry, and send the rich away empty (Luke 1:46-55). In today's scripture text, all stand amazed at the shepherds' report, while Mary "treasured all these words and pondered them in her heart."

In the early eighth century, the Benedictine monk Saint Bede reflected on what he thought Mary knew: "She then knew that the Lord had come in the flesh, whose power is one and eternal with the Father, and he would give to his daughter the church the kingdom of the heavenly Jerusalem. Mary was comparing these things which she had read were to occur with those which she recognized as already having occurred" ("Homilies on the Gospels 1.7").

Whatever Mary knew, her approach is a model for us. Whether or not we know much about the Christ child, we respond best by beholding him, pondering his significance, and embracing him.

Prayer

O God, help us, like Mary, to ponder the significance of your Son's arrival among us, that we may know good news. Amen.

December 27 / Christmas 1

Luke 2:27-32

Simeon came into the temple; and when the parents brought in
the child Jesus, to do for him what was customary under the law,
Simeon took him in his arms and praised God, saying,
"Master, now you are dismissing your servant in peace,
according to your word;
for my eyes have seen your salvation,
which you have prepared in the presence of all peoples,
a light for revelation to the Gentiles
and for glory to your people Israel."

To ponder

Of the Father's love begotten ere the worlds began to be,
he is Alpha and Omega, he the source, the ending he,

of the things that are, that have been, and that future years shall see,
evermore and evermore.
—"Of the Father's love begotten," ELW 295, st. 1

Hope fulfilled

Have you ever seen a long-awaited desire fulfilled? Simeon did.
His prophetic words imply that he believed he would see God's
"salvation" before he died. Now, as he holds the Christ child, he
declares that expectation fulfilled—and praises God.

For Simeon, this event was a long time coming. So are many
of the things God does in our lives. We pray for patience. We ask
for guidance. We pray for a life partner. We pray for healing. We
pray for our children's faith. We ask for help. Sometimes God
answers our prayers quickly. Most of the time, answers come very,
very slowly—if at all. Then again, sometimes the experience of
waiting is more important than the result. And sometimes it is
not our circumstances that are changed by prayer, but us.

What long-awaited hope of yours stands unfulfilled today?
Pray about this. And realize its fulfillment may still not come
quickly. But Simeon's story gives us hope. God does not neglect
the prayers of old (or young) people waiting on God. One day, the
eyes of those who pray will indeed see the salvation of God.

Prayer

O God of our ancestors, give us faith to trust you to show your
salvation in our day, through Christ our Lord. Amen.

December 28 / The Holy Innocents, Martyrs

Matthew 2:13-15

An angel of the Lord appeared to Joseph in a dream and said, "Get up, take the child and his mother, and flee to Egypt, and remain there until I tell you; for Herod is about to search for the child, to destroy him." Then Joseph got up, took the child and his mother by night, and went to Egypt, and remained there until the death of Herod.

To ponder

The children of our world form a window through which we find both the diagnosis and the cure for our sickness. They are first to feel the impacts of our various devastations. . . . According to UNICEF, nearly half of the world's extreme global poor are children.—Cindy Wang Brandt, *Parenting Forward*

Why?

Why do some suffer, while others are saved from suffering?

In today's scripture reading, the child Jesus is saved from certain death. But the dark side of this is the children left behind. As Jesus and his parents depart Bethlehem, a mad tyrant starts a killing spree of children two years old and younger. To boot, Matthew regards both events as fulfilling scripture (2:15, 17-18).

Why did the angel of the Lord not warn *all* families in Bethlehem?

We do not have satisfactory answers to such questions. But we need not look far to find similar questions in our own day: Why is she cured of cancer but I'm not? Why is his prayer answered, but not hers? Why did such an unnecessary accident happen in the first place?

Our scripture passage offers a rather simple word of hope: our God in Christ saves. Even in a world marred by violence and run by tyrants, our God in Christ saves. And this Savior is not naïve to the evil in our world. He has seen it firsthand. Amid violence, terror, and death, Christ shows us a God who is with us and for us, even to the end of the age.

Prayer

O Christ, Emmanuel, hold in your care those who suffer violence, and show us your salvation. Amen.

December 29

Galatians 4:4-6

God sent his Son, born of a woman, born under the law, in order to redeem those who were under the law, so that we might receive adoption as children. And because you are children, God has sent the Spirit of his Son into our hearts, crying, "Abba! Father!"

To ponder

Children have abounding vitality. . . . They always say, "Do it again"; and grown-up [people do] it again until [they are] nearly dead. For grown-up people are not strong enough to exult in monotony. But perhaps God is. . . . God says every morning, "Do it again" to the sun; and every evening, "Do it again" to the moon. . . . For we have sinned and grown old, and our Father is younger than we.—G. K. Chesterton, *Orthodoxy*

Your little ones, dear Lord, are we

No matter how we identify ourselves, we are always someone's child.

We may be a parent. We may be married. We may have siblings. We may have a job. We may come from a significant family. We may occupy an important public role. But at the end of the day, *all* of us are children to someone.

Once we become adults, we rarely identify as anyone's children. We prefer instead to identify ourselves by choices we have made. But God does not view us this way. However successful we become, whatever work we do, whomever we marry or raise, God finally prefers to identify us as children—*God's* children.

Think about this: God really doesn't care that much about your achievements, titles, friendship circles, social creds, and family trophies. They are just not a big a deal in heaven. God really *does* care that you are loved, redeemed, and claimed by Christ. In other words, you belong finally to God. Everything else is just frosting on the cake.

God deeply loves you, just as you are. Nothing else much matters.

Prayer

Holy Spirit, help us to say "Abba! Father!" from our hearts. Help us live from faith, not fear, and from love, not judgment, simply because we are your children, through Christ our Lord. Amen.

December 30

Isaiah 62:1, 3

For Zion's sake I will not keep silent,
and for Jerusalem's sake I will not rest,
until her vindication shines out like the dawn,
and her salvation like a burning torch.

You shall be a crown of beauty in the hand of the LORD,
and a royal diadem in the hand of your God.

To ponder

[Hope] is no longer something we see but rather something we
practice, something we live, something we advocate, something we
plant. At times when we feel as if the world must be coming to an
end tomorrow, our call is not to wait, not to cry, nor to surrender.

Rather, . . . [we] go out today into our garden, into our society, and plant olive trees.—Mitri Raheb, *Bethlehem Besieged*

Hope

We have a lot to learn from ancient Israel about hope.

Israel was never a large nation. It was never a global force. It was never a cultural icon. Most surrounding peoples never gave it a second thought. Even more, when these words from Isaiah were spoken, "Israel" was a hodgepodge band of returned exiles, believing themselves called to restore a fallen Jerusalem. Yet the prophet holds out stubborn hope in the city's vindication by God—though all odds are stacked against it.

This kind of hope is not a fickle wish. Nor is it naïve optimism. It's faith turned toward the future. It's more than a mere feeling, and it's not something we muster up in ourselves by sheer grit. This hope is simply trust in a trustworthy God, a confidence that God's purposes for us will ultimately prevail.

Hopelessness is common in the world today. Many people would have us embrace fear and cynicism instead of hope. But we trust a God who restores exiles, draws near to save, and creates life from death. We are "Jesus people." How can we *not* hope, despite the odds?

Prayer

O Christ, who gives life to the dead: we believe; help our unbelief. In a world marked by hopelessness and fear, help us to hope in you always. Amen.

Revelation 21:1, 3-5

Then I saw a new heaven and a new earth; for the first heaven
and the first earth had passed away, and the sea was no more. . . .
And I heard a loud voice from the throne saying, "See, the home
of God is among mortals. He will dwell with them; they will be
his peoples, and God himself will be with them; he will wipe
every tear from their eyes. Death will be no more; mourning and
crying and pain will be no more, for the first things have passed
away." And the one who was seated on the throne said, "See, I am
making all things new."

To ponder

Finish then thy new creation, pure and spotless let us be;
let us see thy great salvation perfectly restored in thee!

Changed from glory into glory, till in heav'n we take our place,
till we cast our crowns before thee, lost in wonder, love, and praise!
— "Love divine, all loves excelling," ELW 631, st. 4

God at work

As the world marks the end of one year and the beginning of the next, many people are making plans for their personal renewal in the year ahead. But Revelation promises much more than a personal "re-do"—not only a new earth, but even a new heaven.

We are part of an ongoing creation. Astronomers tell us that what we see in a starry sky is in fact very old—the light of stars reaching us after many years. Some of those stars might be extinct by the time their light reaches our eyes. Knowing this does not diminish the wonder of seeing celestial bodies from across the universe.

Scripture promises that God is still at work—on us and on all of creation. Our whole world—our political systems, the natural environment, and even the universe beyond our sight—is subject to God's ongoing, redeeming care. We begin again under the promise received at our baptism: we will be restored by God's great salvation for the whole world.

Prayer

Eternal God, we marvel at your work on all of creation and on us. As we enter a new year, make us mindful of both your tireless work and your endless mercy. Amen.

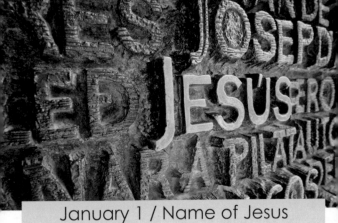

January 1 / Name of Jesus

Philippians 2:9-11

Therefore God also highly exalted him
and gave him the name that is above every name,
so that at the name of Jesus
every knee should bend,
in heaven and on earth and under the earth,
and every tongue should confess
that Jesus Christ is Lord,
to the glory of God the Father.

To ponder

"I wish it need not have happened in my time," said Frodo.

"So do I," said Gandalf, "and so do all who live to see such times. But that is not for them to decide. All we have to decide is what to do with the time that is given us."—J. R. R. Tolkien, *The Fellowship of the Ring*

Born to reign forever

As we enter a new year, self-help articles will offer advice on how to "take control" of our time, as if time is a personal possession that we are given to manage and enhance. But scripture makes a radical claim—that all time is under the rule of Jesus Christ as Lord. God's reign is not strictly about a geographic place or the political kingdoms of this world, but a reign over time itself on earth. Our control is not the issue. We live in time given to us, and that time is ruled by one Lord, Jesus Christ.

This reign of Christ extends even further. It is said that in Roman times, "bending the knee" was a sign of submission to authority, but also a signal that two parties had come to an agreement. The image in Philippians of every knee "in heaven and on earth and under the earth" bending to Jesus shows all creation recognizing Jesus' authority over all things and willingly participating in his reign for the glory of God.

Prayer

Lord God, in Jesus' name we start this new year. Help us remember that all time and space belong to you, so that we live in gratitude for having a part in your gracious plan for the healing of the world. Amen.

January 2

Psalm 148:11-13

Sovereigns of the earth and all peoples,
princes and all rulers of the world;
young men and maidens, old and young together.
Let them praise the name of the LORD,
whose name only is exalted,
whose splendor is over earth and heaven.

To ponder

When I was young I thought dressing for Mass was silly and
empty performance art; now I wonder if it was more a gesture
of something like awe. For great moments in life you prepare
slowly and carefully, and present yourself buffed and polished and

shining, as a way to say something for which we do not yet have particularly good words.—Brian Doyle, *Eight Whopping Lies and Other Stories of Bruised Grace*

All creation sings

We live in times when people long to be recognized. The dutiful modesty of previous generations has been replaced by an anxiety that we will be overlooked or ignored even when we are successful. The nonstop jangle of social media requires that we "curate" our lives at all times, seeking "likes" and followers. We are hungry for praise for ourselves.

The psalms, however, constantly urge us to give praise to God. Is God also hungry for recognition? Or is this a call to remember our humanity? Psalm 148 invites us—young and old, earthly rulers and "all peoples"—to look beyond ourselves and our own concerns, and to see the glory of God.

In Jesus we see God constantly bringing hope and healing, lifting up those who are lowly, and humbling those who are proud. In response we thank and praise God. This might involve loud shouts or murmured prayers or simply the act of preparing to join others in worship. We join the rest of creation in praising God.

Prayer

Gracious God, raise our sights beyond our own concerns, and fill our hearts with gratitude for your love. Teach us to live so that all our words and deeds give you praise. Amen.

January 3 / Christmas 1

John 1:18

No one has ever seen God. It is God the only Son, who is close to the Father's heart, who has made him known.

To ponder

Do not think that I have any serious and final answers to any of the serious and pressing questions of life but do know that I love you with a love ferocious and inarticulate and thorough and mysterious and tidal and always will love you even when you have not as yet picked up the wet towel on the floor which if you do not pick that up soon I am going to roar in such manner that birds in faraway countries will startle and wonder what has shivered the air beneath their holy and extraordinary wings.—Brian Doyle, "Advice to My Son"

Close to the heart

How is the child close to the parent's heart? In infancy the child is literally there, sleeping on her father's chest, or nodding off over his mother's shoulder, the one tiny heart beating right next to the slower thump of the parent's heart.

Then children grow, and the moments of physical closeness wane, but fathers and mothers still feel that closeness like a line of rope vibrating with tension for years on end. Nothing makes a mother's heart race faster than the sound of her own child's cries. As he watches a growing child run a race or sing a solo or spell the word "c-e-m-e-t-e-r-y," a father is sure that everyone in a twenty-foot radius can hear the blood throbbing against his eardrums. *Close* is about so much more than distance.

A loving parent's heart always beats with and for the child no matter how many years pass, no matter how many miles are between them. And God, whose infinite love for the world made the unthinkable leap into finitude, shows us that eternally beating heart of love in Jesus.

Prayer

Loving God, you show us what it means to love unconditionally. Help parents and children everywhere to know what it is to love and be loved, to forgive and be forgiven. Amen.

Matthew 2:1-4

In the time of King Herod, after Jesus was born in Bethlehem of Judea, wise men from the East came to Jerusalem, asking, "Where is the child who has been born king of the Jews? For we observed his star at its rising, and have come to pay him homage." When King Herod heard this, he was frightened, and all Jerusalem with him; and calling together all the chief priests and scribes of the people, he inquired of them where the Messiah was to be born.

To ponder

A miracle is no cute thing but more like the swing of a sword.—Leif Enger, *Peace Like a River*

Searching scripture

The world has returned to its frantic rhythms and, whether or not there was peace at Christmas, the headlines remind us that somewhere in the world now, people are trembling in the shadow of violence. The good news that God reigns among us is bad news to the tyrants of the world who want to claim absolute power.

The story of the magi presents us with two very different uses of scripture. On the one hand, the magi leave their homeland, curious to interpret what they see happening in the world and willing to explore Hebrew prophecy to find out. On the other hand, a Jewish king staying close to home in his fortress is bent on keeping power. Herod wants his sages to read scripture so that he may stay comfortable in his privilege and position.

Why do you read the Bible? Are you open to new ways of seeing God at work in the world, or do you go to the scriptures seeking to hold on to your own comfort and power? Only one way leads to the living God, to the joy of true worship.

Prayer

Holy God, in Jesus your word becomes flesh, and your promise becomes real. Help us to search the scriptures for guidance and truth, to bring hearts of humility and minds open to learn. Amen.

January 5

Matthew 2:9-10

When [the wise men] had heard the king, they set out; and there, ahead of them, went the star that they had seen at its rising, until it stopped over the place where the child was. When they saw that the star had stopped, they were overwhelmed with joy.

To ponder

Look at the stars! look, look up at the skies!
O look at all the fire-folk sitting in the air!
The bright boroughs, the circle-citadels there!
Down in dim woods the diamond delves! the elves'-eyes!
The grey lawns cold where gold, where quickgold lies!
Wind-beat whitebeam! airy abeles set on a flare!
Flake-doves sent floating forth at a farmyard scare!—

Ah well! it is all a purchase, all is a prize.
—Gerard Manley Hopkins, from "The Starlight Night"

Star of wonder

Do you recall looking out the window and noticing that the moon seemed to be following you? From a child's perspective, rarely staying up late enough to see the stars and moon move across the night sky, these bodies might indeed seem to be following you on your journey.

It's unlikely that the magi were that unsophisticated in their evaluation of a new star in the sky. In fact, they were probably far better versed in what ought to be appearing above than the average modern person. And new celestial bodies—comets or supernovas—do indeed appear sometimes. But whether the star of Bethlehem was a natural phenomenon or a supernatural one, the magi realized that this star was notable, and that it required a response. They kept following until they were surprised once again.

What new wonder in your life has made you stop and suspend your daily routines? How often does the wonder of God-with-us move you to join others in worship?

Prayer

Loving God, as the magi saw signs of your promise in the wonders of creation, so teach us to look at all you have made with curiosity. May the vastness and mystery of the universe inspire us to praise you, and to seek your truth in all of life. Amen.

January 6 / Epiphany of Our Lord

Matthew 2:11-12

On entering the house, they saw the child with Mary his mother; and they knelt down and paid him homage. Then, opening their treasure chests, they offered him gifts of gold, frankincense, and myrrh. And having been warned in a dream not to return to Herod, they left for their own country by another road.

To ponder

Eating Jesus, as I did that day to my great astonishment, led me against all my expectations to a faith I'd scorned and work I'd never imagined. . . . In that shocking moment of communion, filled with a deep desire to reach for and become part of a body, I realized that what I'd been doing with my life all along was what I was meant to do: feed people.—Sara Miles, *Take This Bread*

I wonder as I wander

Some of us imagine that worship and growth in faith follow a linear pattern: you are baptized, you learn the basics of the faith, you serve and worship, and you grow. We may be confused when things don't follow this pattern, when our journeys seem to stall out or take unexpected turns. It may be frustrating that growth in faith isn't the simple by-product of following a plan, but it is also great grace that those who have just met Jesus can be moved to sudden and profound worship and service. The wonder of the incarnation is that God in flesh appears among us and, regardless of whether we fully recognize or understand this Jesus, the world is never the same.

The magi started out on a journey that led where they could not have imagined, and they went home again forever changed. Jesus fulfilled a hope and expectation that they had not even realized they had. Likewise, our lives in faith are a mix of intentional journey and surprising stumbles upon wonder. Christ meets us where he has promised to be, and yet God can never be contained there. Thanks be to God that the journey of faith holds mystery and surprise for us all!

Prayer

Holy God, I do not know where I am going, but only that I want you to lead me. I do not know the future, except that you will be present there. Lead me, surprise me, and remind me every day that you hold the future—and me—in your loving hands. Amen.

Household Blessings and Prayers

An evening service of light for Advent

*This brief order may be used on any evening during the season of Advent.
If the household has an Advent wreath (one candle for each of the four
weeks of Advent), it may be lighted during this service. Alternatively, one
simple candle (perhaps a votive candle) may be lighted instead.*

Lighting the Advent wreath

May this candle/these candles be a sign of the coming light of
Christ.
One or more candles may be lighted.

Week 1: Lighting the first candle
Blessed are you, God of Jacob, for you promise to transform
weapons of war into implements of planting and harvest and to

teach us your way of peace; you promise that our night of sin is far gone and that your day of salvation is dawning.

As we light the first Advent candle, wake us from our sleep, wrap us in your light, empower us to live honorably, and guide us along your path of peace.

O house of Jacob, come,
let us walk in the light of the Lord. Amen.

Week 2: Lighting the first two candles
Blessed are you, God of hope, for you promise to bring forth a shoot from the stump of Jesse who will bring justice to the poor, who will deliver the needy and crush the oppressor, who will stand as a signal of hope for all people.

As we light these candles, turn our wills to bear the fruit of repentance, transform our hearts to live in justice and harmony with one another, and fix our eyes on the root of Jesse, Jesus Christ, the hope of all nations.

O people of hope, come,
let us rejoice in the faithfulness of the Lord. Amen.

Week 3: Lighting three candles
Blessed are you, God of might and majesty, for you promise to make the desert rejoice and blossom, to watch over the strangers, and to set the prisoners free.

As we light these candles, satisfy our hunger with your good gifts, open our eyes to the great things you have done for us, and fill us with patience until the coming of the Lord Jesus.

O ransomed people of the Lord, come,
**let us travel on God's holy way
and enter into Zion with singing. Amen.**

Week 4: Lighting all four candles
Blessed are you, God of hosts, for you promised to send a son, Emmanuel, who brought your presence among us; and you promise through your Son Jesus to save us from our sin.

As we light these candles, turn again to us in mercy; strengthen our faith in the word spoken by your prophets; restore us and give us life that we may be saved.

O house of David, come,
**let us rejoice, for the Son of God, Emmanuel,
comes to be with us. Amen.**

Reading
Read the scripture passage printed in the devotion for the day.

Hymn
One of the following hymns may be sung. The hymn might be accompanied by small finger cymbals.

Light one candle to watch for Messiah, ELW 240
People, look east, ELW 248
Savior of the nations, come, ELW 263

During the final seven days of the Advent season (beginning on December 17), the hymn "O come, O come, Emmanuel" (ELW 257) is particularly appropriate. The stanzas of that hymn are also referred to as the "O Antiphons." The first stanza of the hymn could be sung each day during the final days before Christmas in addition to the stanza that is specifically appointed for the day.

First stanza

O come, O come, Emmanuel,
and ransom captive Israel,
that mourns in lonely exile here
until the Son of God appear.
Refrain Rejoice! Rejoice! Emmanuel shall come to you, O Israel.

December 17

O come, O Wisdom from on high,
embracing all things far and nigh:
in strength and beauty come and stay;
teach us your will and guide our way. *Refrain*

December 18

O come, O come, O Lord of might,
as to your tribes on Sinai's height
in ancient times you gave the law
in cloud, and majesty, and awe. *Refrain*

December 19
O come, O Branch of Jesse, free
your own from Satan's tyranny;
from depths of hell your people save,
and give them vict'ry o'er the grave. *Refrain*

December 20
O come, O Key of David, come,
and open wide our heav'nly home;
make safe the way that leads on high,
and close the path to misery. *Refrain*

December 21
O come, O Dayspring, come and cheer;
O Sun of justice, now draw near.
Disperse the gloomy clouds of night,
and death's dark shadow put to flight. *Refrain*

December 22
O come, O King of nations, come,
O Cornerstone that binds in one:
refresh the hearts that long for you;
restore the broken, make us new. *Refrain*

December 23

O come, O come, Emmanuel,
and ransom captive Israel,
that mourns in lonely exile here
until the Son of God appear. *Refrain*

Text: Psalteriolum Cantionum Catholicarum, Köln, 1710; tr. composite
Text sts. 2, 6, 7 © 1997 Augsburg Fortress

Table prayer for Advent

Blessed are you, O Lord our God,
the one who is, who was, and who is to come.
At this table you fill us with good things.
May these gifts strengthen us
to share with the hungry and all those in need,
as we wait and watch for your coming among us
in Jesus Christ our Lord. Amen.

Lighting the Christmas tree

Use this prayer when you first illumine the tree or when you gather at the tree.

Holy God,
we praise you as we light this tree.
It gives light to this place
as you shine light into darkness through Jesus,
the light of the world.

God of all,
we thank you for your love,
the love that has come to us in Jesus.
Be with us now as we remember that gift of love,
and help us to share that love with a yearning world.

Creator God,
you made the stars in the heavens.
Thank you for the light that shines on us in Jesus,
the bright morning star.
Amen.

Blessing of the nativity scene

This blessing may be used when figures are added to the nativity scene and throughout the days of Christmas.

Bless us, O God, as we remember a humble birth. With each angel and shepherd we place here before you, show us the wonder found in a stable. In song and prayer, silence and awe, we adore your gift of love, Christ Jesus our Savior. Amen.

Table prayer for the twelve days of Christmas (December 25-January 5)

With joy and gladness we feast upon your love, O God.
You have come among us in Jesus, your Son,
and your presence now graces this table.
May Christ dwell in us
that we might bear his love to all the world,
for he is Lord forever and ever. Amen.

Blessing for a home at Epiphany

Matthew writes that when the magi saw the shining star stop overhead, they were filled with joy. "On entering the house, they saw the child with Mary his mother" (Matthew 2:11). In the home, Christ is met in family and friends, in visitors and strangers. In the home, faith is shared, nurtured, and put into action. In the home, Christ is welcome.

Twelfth Night (January 5), Epiphany of Our Lord (January 6), or another day during the time after Epiphany offers an occasion for gathering with friends and family members for a blessing for the home. Someone may lead the greeting and blessing, while another person may read the scripture passage. Following an Eastern European tradition, a visual blessing may be inscribed with white chalk above the main door; for example, 20 + CMB + 21. The numbers change with each new year. The three letters stand for either the ancient Latin blessing Christe mansionem benedicat, *which means, "Christ, bless this house," or the legendary names of the magi (Caspar, Melchior, and Balthasar).*

Greeting

Peace to this house and to all who enter here.
By wisdom a house is built,
and through understanding it is established;
through knowledge its rooms are filled
with rare and beautiful treasures. *(Prov. 24:3-4)*

Reading

As we prepare to ask God's blessing on this household,
let us listen to the words of scripture.

In the beginning was the Word,
and the Word was with God, and the Word was God.
He was in the beginning with God.
All things came into being through him,
and without him not one thing came into being.
What has come into being in him was life,
and the life was the light of all people.
The Word became flesh and lived among us, and we have seen
   his glory,
the glory as of a father's only son, full of grace and truth.
From his fullness we have all received, grace upon grace.
(*John 1:1-4, 14, 16*)

Inscription

This inscription may be made with chalk above the entrance:
20 + C M B + 21

Write the appropriate character (left) while speaking the text (right).
The magi of old, known as
C   Caspar,
M   Melchior, and
B   Balthasar,
followed the star of God's Son who came to dwell among us
20   two thousand
21   and twenty-one years ago.
+   Christ, bless this house,
+   and remain with us throughout the new year.

Prayer of Blessing

O God,
you revealed your Son to all people by the shining light of a star.
We pray that you bless this home and all who live here
with your gracious presence.
May your love be our inspiration, your wisdom our guide,
your truth our light, and your peace our benediction;
through Christ our Lord. Amen.

*Then everyone may walk from room to room, blessing the house with
incense or by sprinkling with water, perhaps using a branch from the
Christmas tree.*

Table prayer for Epiphany

Generous God,
you have made yourself known in Jesus, the light of the world.
As this food and drink give us refreshment,
so strengthen us by your spirit,
that as your baptized sons and daughters
we may share your light with all the world.
Grant this through Christ our Lord.
Amen.

Notes

Welcome: Laurentius Laurenti, 1660–1722; tr. Sarah B. Findlater, 1823–1907, "Rejoice, rejoice, believers," ELW 244, st. 4. **November 29:** Alfred Delp, *The Prison Meditations of Father Delp* (Freiburg im Breisgau, Baden-Württemberg, Germany: Herder and Herder, 1968). **November 30:** Phillips Brooks, 1835–1893, "O little town of Bethlehem," ELW 279, st. 3. **December 2:** Martin Luther, *Luther's Small Catechism,* tr. Timothy J. Wengert, study ed. (Minneapolis: Augsburg Fortress, 2016), 31. **December 3:** African American spiritual, "My Lord, what a morning," ELW 438, refrain. **December 6:** Rainer Maria Rilke, *Letters to a Young Poet,* second ed. (Novato, California: New World Library, 2000), 35. **December 7:** Dietrich Bonhoeffer, *Life Together and Prayerbook of the Bible,* Dietrich Bonhoeffer Works, vol. 5 (Minneapolis: Augsburg Fortress, 2004), 38. **December 8:** Johann G. Olearius, 1635–1711, tr. Catherine Winkworth, 1829–1878, "Comfort, comfort now my people," ELW 256, st. 1. **December 9:** Frans Mikael Franzén, 1772–1847, tr. *Lutheran Book of Worship,* "Prepare the royal highway," ELW 264, st. 3. **December 10:** Thomas Merton, *A Book of Hours,* ed. Kathleen Deignan (Notre Dame: Sorin Books, 2007), 147. **December 11:** Ken Untener, "Prophets of a Future Not Our Own," excerpted from a homily drafted for Cardinal John Dearden, 1979. Accessed at www.usccb.org/prayer-and-worship/prayers-and-devotions/prayers/prophets-of-a-future-not-our-own.cfm. **December 12:** John Chrysostom, *Homily 8, St. John Chrysostom on Repentance and Almsgiving,* Fathers of the Church Patristic Series, tr. Gus George Christo (Washington, DC: The Catholic University of America Press, 2005), 115. **December 13:** Irish, 8th cent.; vers. Eleanor H. Hull, 1860–1935, alt.; tr. Mary E. Byrne, 1880–1931, "Be thou my vision," ELW 793, st. 1. **December 14:** Dietrich Bonhoeffer, *Letters and Papers from Prison* (Minneapolis: Augsburg Fortress, 2009), 459. **December 15:** Martin Luther, in *Martin Luther's Christmas Book* (Minneapolis: Augsburg Fortress, 1997), 20. **December 16:** Diana Butler Bass, *Grateful: The Subversive Practice of Giving Thanks* (San Francisco: HarperOne, 2018), 43. **December 17:** James W. Johnson, 1871–1938, "Lift every voice and sing," ELW 841, st. 1. **December 18:** "Let Us Put On the Clothes of Christ," st. 4, *Global Songs 2: Songbook* (Minneapolis: Augsburg Fortress, 1997), © 1993 Bret Hesla, admin. Augsburg Fortress. **December 19:** Carl B. Garve, 1763–1841; tr. Catherine Winkworth, 1829–1878, alt.; "Your Word, O Lord, Is Gentle Dew," *Lutheran Book of Worship* (Augsburg, 1978), 232, st. 1. **December 20:** Alice Walker, "Fundamental Difference," *Revolutionary Petunias and Other Poems* (San Diego: Harcourt & Brace, 1970), 1. **December 21:** Toni Morrison, 1979 Commencement Speech, Barnard College, New York, New York. **December 22:** bell hooks and John Perry Barlow talk 'prana in cyberspace,'" February 8, 2018, Lion's Roar website. Accessed at www.lionsroar.com/bell-hooks-talks-to-john-perry-barlow. **December 23:** Zora Neale Hurston, *Their Eyes Were Watching God,* 75th anniversary ed. (New York: Amistad, 2006). **December**

24: Joseph Mohr, 1792–1849; tr. John F. Young, 1820–1885, "Silent night, holy night," ELW 281, st. 3. **December 25:** Martin Luther, "Sermon on the Afternoon of Christmas Day" (1530), *Luther's Works*, vol. 51, ed. and trans. John W. Doberstein (Philadelphia: Muhlenberg Press, 1959), 217. Martin Luther, "Brief Instruction on What to Look For and Expect in the Gospels" (1521), *Luther's Works*, vol. 35, ed. and trans. John W. Doberstein (Philadelphia: Muhlenberg Press, 1959), 119. **December 26:** Polish carol, tr. Edith M. G. Reed, 1885–1933, "Infant holy, infant lowly," ELW 276, st. 1. The Venerable Bede, "Homilies on the Gospels 1.7," *Ancient Christian Commentary on Scripture. New Testament III: Luke*, ed. Arthur A. Just Jr. (Downers Grove, IL: InterVarsity, 2003), 43. **December 27:** Marcus Aurelius Clemens Prudentius, 348–413, "Of the Father's love begotten," ELW 295, st. 1. **December 28:** Cindy Wang Brandt, *Parenting Forward: How to Raise Children with Justice, Mercy, and Kindness* (Grand Rapids: Eerdmans, 2019), 2–3. **December 29:** G. K. Chesterton, *Orthodoxy* (Wheaton, IL: Harold Shaw, 1994), 61. **December 30:** Mitri Raheb, *Bethlehem Besieged: Stories of Hope in Times of Trouble* (Minneapolis: Fortress, 2004), 157. **December 31:** Charles Wesley, 1707–1788, "Love divine, all loves excelling," ELW 631, st. 4. **January 1:** J. R. R. Tolkien, *The Fellowship of the Ring* (New York: Ballantine, 1965), 82. **January 2:** Brian Doyle, *Eight Whopping Lies and Other Stories of Bruised Grace* (Cincinnati: Franciscan Media, 2017), 119. **January 3:** Brian Doyle, "Advice to My Son," in *Grace Notes* (Chicago: Acta Publications, 2011), 22. **January 4:** Leif Enger, *Peace Like a River* (New York: Grove Atlantic, 2001), 4. **January 5:** Gerard Manley Hopkins, from "The Starlight Night" in *Gerard Manley Hopkins: The Major Works*, Oxford World's Classics (New York: Oxford University Press, 1986), 128. **January 6:** Sara Miles, *Take This Bread: A Radical Conversion* (New York: Ballantine, 2007), xiii.